MAPS

Pebb

T0084927

What Is a Map?

by
Jennifer M. Besel

Consulting editor:
Gail Saunders-Smith, PhD

Consultant:
Dr. Sarah E. Battersby
Department of Geography
University of South Carolina

CAPSTONE PRESS
a capstone imprint

Pebble Books are published by Capstone Press,
1710 Roe Crest Drive, North Mankato, Minnesota 56003
www.capstonepub.com

Library of Congress Cataloging-in-Publication Data
Besel, Jennifer M.
What is a map? / by Jennifer M. Besel.
pages cm—(Pebble Books. Maps)
Includes bibliographical references and index.
Summary: "Simple text with full-color photos and illustrations provide basic
information about maps"—Provided by publisher.
ISBN 978-1-4765-3081-9 (library binding)—ISBN 978-1-4765-3503-6 (ebook pdf)—
ISBN 978-1-4765-3521-0 (paperback)
1. Maps—Juvenile literature. I. Title.
GA105.6.B48 2014
912—dc23   2012046454

Editorial Credits
Gene Bentdahl, designer; Kathy McColley, production specialist; Sarah Schuette,
photo stylist; Marcy Morin, scheduler

Photo Credits
Capstone: 9, 11, 13, 15; Capstone Studio: Karon Dubke, cover, 1, 5, 7, 17, 19, 21

Note to Parents and Teachers

The Maps set supports social studies standards related to people, places, and
environments. This book describes and illustrates maps. The images support early
readers in understanding the text. The repetition of words and phrases helps early
readers learn new words. This book also introduces early readers to subject-specific
vocabulary words, which are defined in the Glossary section. Early readers may
need assistance to read some words and to use the Table of Contents, Glossary, Read
More, Internet Sites, and Index sections of the book.

Table of Contents

Finding Your Way

Imagine you're on
a family trip. Oh, no!
You missed the turn.
Which way should you go?
Grab a map!

Maps are tools
that help you find your way.
Maps and globes show
what the world looks like
from above.

7

Every map shows an area
of Earth. Some maps show
streets and buildings.
Other maps show mountains
and lakes.

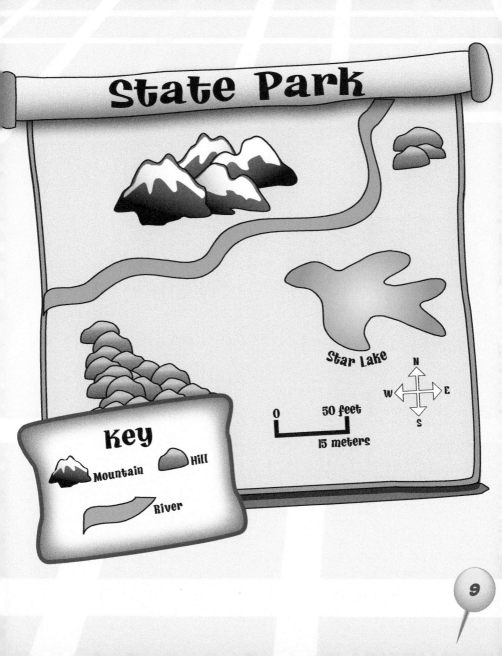

State Park

Star Lake

N
W — E
S

0   50 feet
15 meters

Key

Mountain   Hill

River

9

Map Features

All maps have a compass rose. The compass rose shows which direction is north, south, east, or west.

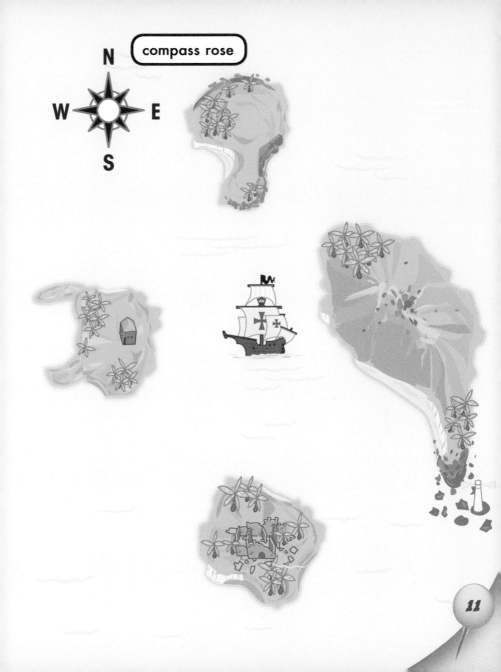

compass rose

Map symbols

stand for real places.

A blue line stands for a river.

Look at the key to see

what the symbols mean.

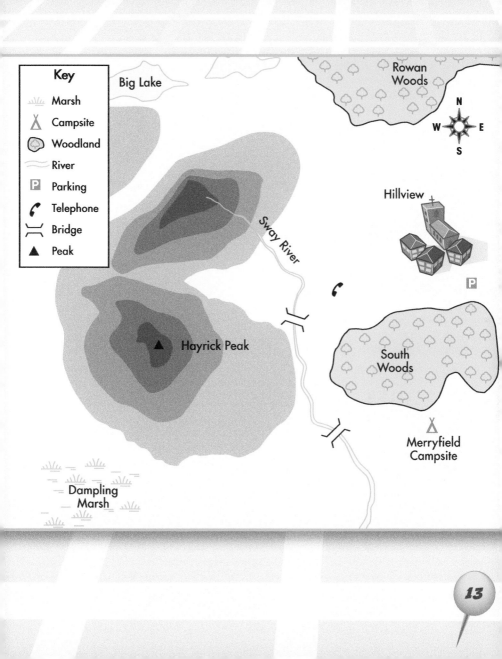

Key

Marsh
Campsite
Woodland
River
Parking
Telephone
Bridge
Peak

Big Lake

Rowan Woods

N
W   E
S

Hillview

Sway River

P

Hayrick Peak

South Woods

Dampling Marsh

Merryfield Campsite

Places are drawn small enough to fit on a map. A map scale tells you what a distance on the map equals on Earth.

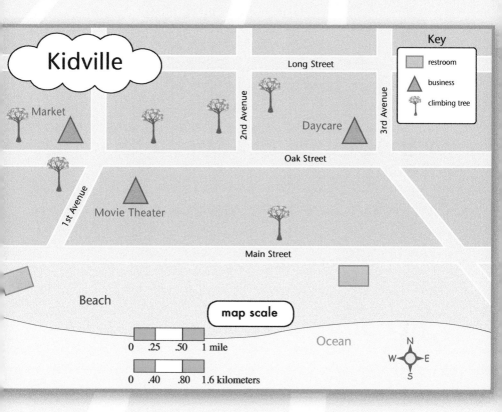

Kidville

Key
- restroom
- business
- climbing tree

Long Street

Market

2nd Avenue

3rd Avenue

Daycare

Oak Street

1st Avenue

Movie Theater

Main Street

Beach

map scale

0   .25   .50   1 mile

0   .40   .80   1.6 kilometers

Ocean

N
W   E
S

Using Maps

People have used maps for thousands of years. Many old maps show the routes ships used to get from one place to another.

GÉOGRAPHIE primitive DES GRECS.

HÉSIODE, HOMÈRE, ORPHÉE,
neuf siècles avant notre ère.

VOYAGES DES ARGONAUTES
ET D' ULYSSE.

CÔTÉ DE LA NUIT (ΠΡΟΣ ΖΟΦΟΝ Homer)
plus tard EUROPE

CÔTÉ DU JOUR (ΠΡΟΣ ΗΩ' Η' ΛΙΟΝ ΤΕ Homer)
plus tard ASIE

Today maps are made with computers. GPS systems show maps of where you are and maps of where you are going.

There's a map for
almost every place on Earth.
Use a map, and you can
always find your way!

Grand Canyon National Park

Glossary

compass rose—a label that shows direction on a map

direction—the way that someone or something is moving or pointing

globe—a round model of the world

GPS—an electronic tool used to find the location of an object; GPS stands for global positioning system

key—a list or chart that explains symbols on a map or graph

route—the regular path you follow to go somewhere

scale—a map tool that compares distances on a map to real distances on Earth

symbol—an object that stands for something else

Read More

Besel, Jennifer M. *Types of Maps.* Maps. Mankato, Minn.: Capstone Press, 2014.

Greve, Meg. *Maps Are Flat, Globes Are Round.* Little World Geography. Vero Beach, Fla.: Rourke Pub., 2010.

Spilsbury, Louise. *Mapping.* Investigate. Chicago: Heinemann Library, 2010.

Internet Sites

FactHound offers a safe, fun way to find Internet sites related to this book. All of the sites on FactHound have been researched by our staff.

Here's all you do:

Visit *www.facthound.com*

Type in this code: 9781476530819

Check out projects, games and lots more at
www.capstonekids.com

Critical Thinking Using the Common Core

1. Describe the features found on every map. What purpose does each feature serve? (Craft and Structure)

2. Map symbols stand for real places. What are some different meanings for the words "stand for?" (Craft and Structure)

3. Compare the maps on pages 17 and 19. Even though one map is very old and the other is new, what similarities do these maps have? Do you think that most maps have things in common, regardless of age? If so, why? If not, why not? (Craft and Structure)

Index

Word Count: 181
Grade: 1
Early-Intervention Level: 17